THE END OF
CORPORATE
IMPERIALISM

Harvard Business Review

CLASSICS

THE END OF CORPORATE IMPERIALISM

C.K. Prahalad and
Kenneth Lieberthal

Harvard Business Press
Boston, Massachusetts

Copyright 2008 Harvard Business School Publishing Corporation
Originally published in *Harvard Business Review* in August 2003
Reprint #R0308G
All rights reserved
Printed in the United States of America

12 11 10 09 08   5 4 3 2 1

No part of this publication may be reproduced, stored in or introduced into a retrieval system, or transmitted, in any form, or by any
means (electronic, mechanical, photocopying, recording, or other-
wise), without the prior permission of the publisher. Requests for
permission should be directed to permissions@hbsp.harvard.edu,
or mailed to Permissions, Harvard Business School Publishing, 60
Harvard Way, Boston, Massachusetts 02163.

ISBN 978-1-4221-7973-4

Library-of-Congress cataloging information forthcoming

The paper used in this publication meets the requirements of the
American National Standard for Permanence of Paper for Publica-
tions and Documents in Libraries and Archives Z39.48-1992.

THE
HARVARD BUSINESS REVIEW
CLASSICS SERIES

Since 1922, *Harvard Business Review* has been a leading source of breakthrough ideas in management practice—many of which still speak to and influence us today. The HBR Classics series now offers you the opportunity to make these seminal pieces a part of your permanent management library. Each volume contains a groundbreaking idea that has shaped best practices and inspired countless managers around the world—and will change how you think about the business world today.

THE END OF
CORPORATE
IMPERIALISM

s they search for growth, multinational corporations will have to compete in the big emerging markets of China, India, Indonesia, and Brazil. The operative word is "emerging." A vast consumer base of hundreds of millions of people is developing rapidly. Despite the uncertainty and the difficulty of doing business in markets that remain opaque to outsiders, Western MNCs will have no choice but to enter them. (See the table "Market

Size: Emerging Markets Versus the United States.")

During the first wave of market entry in the 1980s, MNCs operated with what might be termed an imperialist mind-set. They assumed that the big emerging markets were new markets for their old products. They foresaw a bonanza in incremental sales for their existing products or the chance to squeeze profits out of their sunset technologies. Further, the corporate center was seen as the sole locus of product and process innovation. Many multinationals did not consciously look at emerging markets as sources of technical and managerial talent for their global operations. As a result of this imperialist mind-set, multinationals have achieved only limited success in those markets.

Many corporations, however, are beginning to see that the opportunity big emerging markets represent will demand a new way of thinking. Success will require more than simply developing greater cultural sensitivity. The more we understand the nature of these markets, the more we believe that multinationals will have to rethink and reconfigure every element of their business models.

So while it is still common today to question how corporations like General Motors and McDonald's will change life in the big emerging markets, Western executives would be smart to turn the question around. Success in the emerging markets will require innovation and resource shifts on such a scale that life within the multinationals themselves will inevitably be transformed. In short, as MNCs achieve success in those markets, they will also bring corporate imperialism to an end.

We would not like to give the impression that we think markets such as China, India, Brazil, and Indonesia will enjoy clear sailing. As Indonesia is showing, these markets face major obstacles to continued high growth; political disruptions, for example, can slow down and even reverse trends toward more open markets. But given the long-term growth prospects, MNCs will have to compete in those markets. Having studied in depth the evolution of India and China over the past 20 years, and having worked extensively with MNCs competing in these and other countries, we believe that there are five basic questions that MNCs must answer to compete in the big emerging markets:

- Who is the emerging middle-class market in these countries, and what kind of business model will effectively serve their needs?

- What are the key characteristics of the distribution networks in these markets, and how are the networks evolving?

- What mix of local and global leadership is required to foster business opportunities?

- Should the MNC adopt a consistent strategy for all its business units within one country?

- Will local partners accelerate the multinational's ability to learn about the market?

WHAT IS THE BUSINESS MODEL FOR THE EMERGING MIDDLE CLASS?

What is big and emerging in countries like China and India is a new consumer base consisting of hundreds of millions of people. Starved of choice for over 40 years, the rising middle class is hungry for consumer goods and a better quality of life and is ready to spend. The emerging markets have entered a new era of product availability and choice. In India alone, there are 50 brands of toothpaste available today and more than 250 brands of shoes.

Consumers are experimenting and changing their choice of products rapidly. Indians, for example, will buy any product once, and brand switching is common. One survey found that Indian consumers tried on average 6.2 brands of the same packaged goods product in one year, compared with 2.0 for American consumers. But does this growth of consumer demand add up to a wealth of opportunity for the MNCs?

The answer is yes . . . but. Consider the constitution of the middle class itself. When managers in the West hear about the emerging middle class of India or China, they tend to think in terms of the middle class in Europe or the United States. This is one sign of an imperialist mind-set—the assumption that everyone must be just like us. True, consumers in the emerging markets today are much more affluent than they were before their countries liberalized trade, but they are not affluent by Western standards. This is usually the first big miscalculation that MNCs make.

When these markets are analyzed, moreover, they turn out to have a structure very unlike those of the West. Income levels that characterize the Western middle class would represent a tiny upper class of consumers in any of the emerging markets. Today the active consumer market in the big emerging markets has a three-tiered pyramid structure. (See the exhibit "The Market Pyramid in China, India, and Brazil.")

Consider India. At the top of the pyramid, in tier one, is a relatively small number of consumers who are responsive to international brands and have the income to afford them. Next comes tier two, a much larger group of people who are less attracted to international brands. Finally, at the bottom of the pyramid of consumers is tier three—a massive group that is loyal to local customs, habits, and often to local brands. Below that is another huge group made up of people who are unlikely to become active consumers anytime soon.

MNCs have tended to bring their existing products and marketing strategies to the emerging markets without properly accounting for these market pyramids. They end up, therefore, becoming high-end niche players. That's what happened to Revlon, for example, when it introduced its Western beauty products to China in 1976 and to India in 1994. Only the top tier valued and could afford the cachet of Revlon's brand. And consider Ford's recent foray into India with its Escort, which Ford priced at more than $21,000. In India, anything over $20,000 falls into the luxury segment. The most popular car, the Maruti Suzuki, sells for $10,000 or less. Fiat learned to serve that tier of the market in Brazil, designing a new model called the Palio specifically for Brazilians. Fiat is now poised to transfer that success from Brazil to India.

While it is seductive for companies like Ford to think of big emerging markets as new outlets for old products, a mind-set focused on incremental volume misses the real opportunity. To date, MNCs like Ford and

Revlon have either ignored tier two of the pyramid or conceded it to local competitors. But if Ford wants to be more than a small, high-end player, it will have to design a robust and roomy $9,000 car to compete with Fiat's Palio or with a locally produced car.

Tailoring products to the big emerging markets is not a trivial task. Minor cultural adaptations or marginal cost reductions will not do the job. Instead, to overcome an implicit imperialism, companies must undergo a fundamental rethinking of every element of their business model.

Rethinking the Price/Performance Equation

Consumers in big emerging markets are getting a fast education in global standards, but they often are unwilling to pay global prices. In India, an executive in a multinational food-processing company told us the story of a man in Delhi who went to McDonald's for a hamburger. He didn't like the food or the prices, but he liked the ambience. Then he went to Nirula's, a successful Delhi food chain. He liked the food and the prices there, but he complained to the manager because Nirula's did not have the same pleasant atmosphere as McDonald's. The moral of the story? Price/performance expectations are changing, often to the consternation of both the multinationals and the locals. McDonald's has been forced to adapt its menu to local tastes by adding vegetable burgers. Local chains like Nirula's have been pushed to meet global standards for cleanliness and ambience.

Consumers in the big emerging markets are far more focused than their Western counterparts on the price/performance equation. That focus tends to give low-cost local competitors the edge in hotly contested markets. MNCs can, however, learn to turn this price sensitivity to their advantage.

Philips Electronics, for example, introduced a combination video-CD player in China in 1994. Although there is virtually no market for this product in Europe or the United States, the Chinese quickly embraced it as a great two-for-one bargain. More than 15 million units have been sold in China, and the product seems likely to catch on in

Indonesia and India. Consumers in those countries see the player as good value for the money.

Rethinking Brand Management

Armed with their powerful, established brands, multinationals are likely to overestimate the extent of Westernization in the emerging markets and the value of using a consistent approach to brand management around the world.

In India, Coca-Cola overvalued the pull of its brand among the tier-two consumers. Coke based its advertising strategy on its worldwide image and then watched the advantage slip to Pepsi, which had adopted a campaign that was oriented toward the Indian market. As one of Coke's senior executives recently put it in the *Wall Street Journal*, "We're so successful in international business that we applied a tried-and-true formula . . . and it was the wrong formula to apply in India."

It took Coke more than two years to get the message, but it is now repositioning itself by using local heroes, such as popular cricket players, in its advertising. Perhaps more important, it is heavily promoting a popular Indian brand of cola—Thums Up—which Coke bought from a local bottler in 1993 only to scorn it for several years as a poor substitute for the Real Thing.

Rethinking the Costs of Market Building

For many MNCs, entering an emerging market means introducing a new product or service category. But Kellogg, for example, found that introducing breakfast cereals to India was a slow process because it meant creating new eating habits. Once the company had persuaded Indians to eat cereal, at great expense, local competitors were able to ride on Kellogg's coattails by introducing breakfast cereals with local flavors. As a result, Kellogg may discover in the long run that it paid too high a price for too small a market. Sampling, celebrity endorsements, and other forms of consumer education are expensive: Regional tastes vary, and language barriers can create difficulties. India, for example, has more than a dozen major languages and pronounced cultural differences across regions.

Multinationals would do well to rethink the costs of building markets. Changing developed habits is difficult and expensive. Providing consumers with a new product that requires no reeducation can be much easier. For example, consider the rapid adoption of pagers in China. Because telephones are not widely available there, pagers have helped fill the void as a means of one-way communication.

Rethinking Product Design

Even when consumers in emerging markets appear to want the same products as are sold elsewhere, some redesign is often necessary to reflect differences in use and distribution. Because the Chinese use pagers to send entire messages—which is not how they were intended to be used—Motorola developed pagers capable of displaying more lines of information. The result: Motorola encountered the enviable problem of having to scramble to keep up with exploding demand for its product.

In the mid-1980s, a leading MNC in telecommunications began exporting its electronic switching system to China for use in the phone system. The switching system had been designed for the company's home market, where there were many customers but substantial periods when the phones were not in use. In China, on the other hand, there were very few phones, but they were in almost constant use. The switching system, which worked flawlessly in the West, simply couldn't handle the load in China. Ultimately, the company had to redesign its software.

Distribution can also have a huge impact on product design. A Western maker of frozen desserts, for example, had to reformulate one of its products not because of differences in consumers' tastes but because the refrigerators in most retail outlets in India weren't cold enough to store the product properly. The product had been designed for storage at minus 15 degrees centigrade, but the typical retailer's refrigerator operates at minus four degrees. Moreover, power interruptions frequently shut down the refrigerators.

Rethinking Packaging

Whether the problem is dust, heat, or bumpy roads, the distribution infrastructure in emerging markets places special strains on packaging. One glass manufacturer, for example, was stunned at the breakage it sustained as a result of poor roads and trucks in India.

And consumers in tiers two and three are likely to have packaging preferences that are different from consumers in the West. Single-serve packets, or sachets, are enormously popular in India. They allow consumers to buy only what they need, experiment with new products, and conserve cash at the same time. Products as varied as detergents, shampoos, pickles, cough syrup, and oil are sold in sachets in India, and it is estimated that they make up 20% to 30% of the total sold in their categories. Sachets are spreading as a marketing device for such items as shampoos in China as well.

Rethinking Capital Efficiency

The common wisdom is that the infra-structure problems in emerging markets—inefficient distribution systems, poor banking facilities, and inadequate logistics—will require companies to use more capital than in Western markets, not less. But that is the wrong mind-set. Hindustan Lever, a sub-sidiary of Unilever in India, saw a low-cost Indian detergent maker, Nirma, become the largest branded detergent maker in the world over a seven-year period by courting the tier-two and tier-three markets. Realizing that it could not compete by making marginal changes, Hindustan Lever rethought every aspect of its business, including production, distribution, marketing, and capital efficiency.

Today Hindustan Lever operates a $2 billion business with effectively zero working capital. Consider just one of the practices that makes this possible. The company keeps a supply of signed checks from its dealers. When it ships an order, it simply writes in the correct amount for the order. This practice is not uncommon in India. The Indian agribusiness company, Rallis, uses it with its 20,000 dealers in rural India. But this way of doing things is unheard of in Unilever's home countries—the United Kingdom and the Netherlands.

Hindustan Lever also manages to operate with minimal fixed capital. It does so in part through an active program of supplier management; the company works with local entrepreneurs who own and manage plants whose capacity is dedicated to Hindustan Lever's products. Other MNCs will find that there is less need for vertical integration in emerging markets than they might think. Quality suppliers can be located and developed. Their lower overhead structure can help the MNCs gain a competitive cost position. Supply chain management is an important tool for changing the capital efficiency of a multinational's operations.

Rather than concede the market, Hindustan Lever radically changed itself and is today successfully competing against Nirma with a low-cost detergent called Wheel. The lesson learned in India has not been lost on

Unilever. It is unlikely to concede tier-two and tier-three markets in China, Indonesia, or Brazil without a fight.

HOW DOES THE DISTRIBUTION SYSTEM WORK?

One of the greatest regrets of multinational executives, especially those we spoke with in China, was that they had not invested more in distribution before launching their products. Access to distribution is often critical to success in emerging markets, and it cannot be taken for granted. There is no substitute for a detailed understanding of the unique characteristics of a market's distribution system and how that system is likely to evolve.

Consider the differences between China and India. Distribution in China is primarily local and provincial. Under the former planned economy, most distribution networks were confined to political units, such as counties, cities, or provinces. Even at present there is no real national distribution network for most products. Many MNCs have gained access to provincial networks by creating joint ventures. But these are now impediments to the creation of the badly needed national network; Chinese joint-venture partners protect their turf. This gap between the MNCs' need for a national, cost-effective distribution system and the more locally oriented goals of their partners is creating serious tensions. We expect that many joint ventures formed originally to allow multi-nationals to have market and distribution access will be restructured because of this very issue during the next five to seven years.

In India, on the other hand, individual entrepreneurs have already put together a national distribution system in a wide variety of businesses. Established companies such as Colgate-Palmolive and Godrej in personal care, Hindustan Lever in packaged goods, Tatas in trucks, Bajaj in scooters—the list is long—control their own distribution systems. Those systems take the form of long-standing arrangements with networks of small-scale distributors throughout the country, and the banking network is part of those relationships. Many of the established packaged goods companies reach more than 3 million retail outlets—using trains, trucks, bullock-drawn carts, camels, and bicycles. And many companies claim to service each one of those outlets once a week.

Nevertheless, any MNC that wants to establish its own distribution system in India inevitably runs up against significant obstacles and costs. Ford, for example, is trying to establish a new, high-quality dealer network to sell cars in India. To obtain a dealership, each prospective dealer is expected to invest a large amount of his own money and must undergo special training. In the long haul, Ford's approach may prove to be a major source of advantage to the company, but the cost in cash and managerial attention of building the dealers' network will be substantial.

Ironically, the lack of a national distribution system in China may be an advantage. MNCs with patience and ingenuity can more easily build distribution systems to suit their needs, and doing so might confer competitive advantages. As one manager we talked to put it, "The trick to sustained, long-term profitability in China lies not in technology or in savvy advertising or even in low pricing but rather in building a modern distribution system." Conceivably, China may see consolidation of the retail market earlier than India.

The Chinese and Indian cases signal the need for MNCs to develop a market-specific distribution strategy. In India, MNCs will have to determine who controls national distribution in order to distinguish likely partners from probable competitors. In China, multinationals seeking national distribution of their products must consider the motivations of potential partners before entering relationships that may frustrate their intentions.

WILL LOCAL OR EXPATRIATE LEADERSHIP BE MORE EFFECTIVE?

Leadership of a multinational's venture in an emerging market requires a complex blend of local sensitivity and global knowledge. Getting the balance right is critical but never easy. MNCs frequently lack the cultural understanding to get the mix of expatriate and local leaders right.

Expatriates from the multinational's host country play multiple roles. They transfer technology and management practices. They ensure that local employees understand and practice the corporate culture. In the early stages of market development, expatriates are the conduits for information flow between the multinational's corporate office and the local operation. But while headquarters staffs usually recognize the importance of sending information to the local operation, they tend to be less aware that information must also be received from the other direction. Expatriates provide credibility at headquarters when they convey information, especially information concerning the adaptations the corporation must make in order to be successful in the emerging market. Given these important roles, the large number of expatriates in China—170,000 by one count—is understandable.

Every multinational operation we observed in China had several expatriates in management positions. In India, by contrast, we rarely saw expatriate managers, and the few that we did see were usually of Indian origin. That's because among the big emerging markets, India is unique in that it has developed, over time, a cadre of engineers and managers. The Indian institutes of technology and institutes of management turn out graduates with a high degree of technical competence.

Perhaps more important from the perspective of a multinational, Indian managers speak English fluently and seem adept at learning new corporate cultures. At the same time, they have a much better appreciation of local nuances and a deeper commitment to the Indian market than any expatriate manager could have.

Those seeming advantages may be offset, however, by two disadvantages. First, a management team of native-born managers may not have the same share of voice at corporate headquarters that expatriate managers have. Yet maintaining a strong voice is essential, given the difficulty most managers at corporate headquarters have in understanding the dynamics and peculiar requirements of operating in emerging markets. Second, the "soft technology" that is central to Western competitive advantage—the bundle of elements that creates a market-sensitive, cost-effective, dynamic organization—is hard to develop when the management team consists of people who have worked only briefly, if at all, in such an organization.

Several multinationals have sent expatriates of Chinese or Indian origin from their U.S. or European base back to their Chinese or Indian operations in order to convey the company's soft technology in a culturally sensitive way. But that strategy has not, in general, been successful. As one manager we spoke to noted, "Indians from the United States who are sent back as expatriates are frozen in time. They remember the India they left 20 years ago. They are totally out of sync. But they do not have the humility to accept that they have to learn." We heard the same sentiment echoed in China, both for Chinese-Americans and, less frequently, for

Chinese who had obtained a higher education in the United States and then returned as part of a multinational management team.

Using American or West European expatriates during the early years of market entry can make sense, but this approach has its own set of problems. Cultural and language difficulties in countries like China and India typically limit expats' interaction with the locals as well as their effectiveness. In addition, the need to understand how to deal with the local political system, especially in China, makes long-term assignments desirable. It often takes an expatriate manager two years to get fully up to speed. From the company's perspective, it makes sense to keep that manager in place for another three years to take full advantage of what he or she has learned. But few Western expatriates are willing to stay in China that long; many feel that a long assignment keeps them out of the loop and may impose a high career cost. Multinationals, therefore, need to think about how to attract and retain high-quality expatriate talent, how to maintain expats' links to the parent company, and how to use and pass along expats' competencies once they move on to other assignments.

IS IT NECESSARY TO PRESENT ONE FACE?

Beyond the normal organizational questions that would exist wherever a company does business, there is a question of special importance in emerging markets: Do local political considerations require the multinational to adopt a uniform strategy for each of its business units operating in the country, or can it permit each unit to act on its own?

Again, the contrasts between China and India make clear why there is no one right answer to this question. In China, massive governmental interference in the economy makes a uniform country strategy necessary. The Chinese government tends to view the activities of individual business units as part of a single company's effort, and therefore concessions made by any one unit—such as an agreement to achieve a certain level of local sourcing—may well become requirements for the others. An MNC in China must be able to articulate a set of principles that conforms to China's announced priorities, and it should coordinate the activities of its various business units so that they resonate with those priorities.

But given the way most multinationals operate, presenting one face to China is very difficult. Business units have their own P&L responsibilities and are reluctant to lose their autonomy. Reporting lines can become overly complex. Although we observed many organizational approaches, not a single MNC we looked at is completely satisfied with its approach to this difficult issue.

Is it any wonder? Consider the life of one MNC executive we visited in China. As the head of his company's China effort, he has to coordinate with the company's regional headquarters in Japan, report to international headquarters in Europe, and maintain close contact with corporate headquarters in North America. He also has to meet with members of the Chinese government, with the MNC's business unit executives in China, and with the leaders of the business units' Chinese partners. Simply maintaining all of these contacts is extraordinarily taxing and time consuming.

There is somewhat less need to present one face to India. Since 1991, the Indian government has scaled back its efforts to shape what MNCs do in the country. Business units may therefore act more independently than would be appropriate in China. The strategy for India can be developed on a business-by-business basis. Nonetheless, the market is large and complex. National regulations are onerous, and state-level governments are still so different from one another that MNCs are well advised to develop knowledge that they can share with all their business units in India.

DO PARTNERS FOSTER VALUABLE LEARNING?

In the first wave of market entry, multinationals used joint ventures extensively as a way not only to navigate through bureaucratic processes but also to learn about new markets. With few exceptions, however, joint ventures in emerging markets have been problematic. In some cases, executives of the multinationals mistakenly thought the joint venture would do their strategic thinking for them. In most cases, tensions in joint venture relationships have diverted management attention away from learning about the market.

One consistent problem is that each party enters the joint venture with very different expectations. One Chinese manager described the situation in terms of an old saying: "We are sleeping in the same bed with different dreams." The local partner sees the MNC as a source of technology and investment, and the multinational sees the partner as a means of participating in the domestic market.

When they come to an emerging market, multinationals are usually building manufacturing and marketing infrastructures, and they don't expect immediate returns. Local partners, however, often want to see short-term profit. This disparity of aims leads to enormous strain in the relationship. The costs associated with expatriate managers also become a bone of contention. Who controls what can be yet another source of trouble—especially when the domestic partner has experience in the business. And when new investment is needed to grow the business, local partners often are unable to bring in the matching funds, yet they resent the dilution of their holding and the ensuing loss of control.

MNCs are finally learning that their local partners often do not have adequate market knowledge. The experience of most local partners predates the emergence of real consumer markets, and their business practices can be archaic. As markets evolve toward greater transparency, as MNCs develop senior managers who understand how the system works, and as the availability of local talent increases, multinationals have less to gain by using intermediaries as a vehicle for learning.

The MNCs' need for local partners is already diminishing. In 1997, a consulting firm surveyed 67 companies invested in China and found that the percentage of their projects that became wholly foreign-owned enterprises grew steadily from 18% in 1992 to 37% in 1996. A passive partner that can provide a local face may still be important in some industries, but this is a very different matter from a joint venture.

SUCCESS WILL TRANSFORM THE MULTINATIONALS

As executives look for growth in the big emerging markets, they tend quite naturally to focus on the size of the opportunity and the challenges that lie ahead. Few stop to think about how success will transform their companies. But consider the magnitude of the changes we have been describing and the sheer size of the markets in question. Success in the big emerging markets will surely change the shape of the modern multinational as we know it today.

For years, executives have assumed they could export their current business models around the globe. That assumption has to change. Citicorp, for example, aims to serve a billion banking customers by 2010. There is no way Citicorp, given its current cost structure, can profitably serve someone in Beijing or Delhi whose net wealth is less than $5,000. But if Citicorp creates a new business model—rethinking every element of its cost structure—it will be able to serve not only average Chinese people but also inner-city residents in New York. In short, companies must realize that the innovation required to serve the large tier-two and tier-three segments in emerging markets has the potential to make them more competitive in their traditional markets—and therefore in all markets.

Over time, the imperialist assumption that innovation comes from the center will gradually fade away and die. Increasingly, as multinationals develop products better adapted to the emerging markets, they are finding that those markets are becoming an important source of innovation. Telecommunications companies, for example, are discovering that people in markets with no old technology to forget may accept technological changes faster. MNCs such as Texas Instruments and Motorola are assigning responsibility for software-oriented business development to their Indian operations. China has become such a significant market for video-CD players that the Chinese are likely to be major players in introducing the next round of video-CD standards around the world.

The big emerging markets will also have a significant influence on the product development philosophy of the MNCs. One major multinational recognized to its surprise that the Chinese have found a way of producing high-quality detergents with equipment and processes that cost about one-fifth of what the MNC spends. Stories like that can be repeated in a wide variety of businesses, including cement, textile machinery, trucks, and television sets.

As product development becomes decentralized, collaboration between labs in Bangalore, London, and Dallas, for example, will gradually become the rule, not the exception. New product introductions will have to take into consideration nontraditional centers of influence. Thus in the CD business at Philips, new product introductions, which previously occurred almost exclusively in Europe, now also take place in Shanghai and California.

As corporate imperialism draws to a close, multinationals will increasingly look to emerging markets for talent. India is already recognized as a source of technical talent in engineering, sciences, and software, as well as in some aspects of management. High-tech companies recruit in India not only for the Indian market but also for the global market. China, given its growth and its technical and management-training infrastructure, has not yet reached that stage, but it may well reach it in the not-too-distant future.

A major shift in geographical resources will take place within the next five years. Philips is already downsizing in Europe and reportedly employs more Chinese than Dutch workers. Over 40% of the market for Coca-Cola, Gillette, Lucent, Boeing, and GE Power Systems is in Asia. And in the last two years, ABB has shrunk its European workforce by more than 40,000 while adding 45,000 people in Asia.

In addition to these changes, an increasing percentage of the investment in marketing and in plant and equipment will go to the emerging markets. As those markets grow to account for 30% to 40% of capital invested—and even a larger percentage of market share and profits—they will attract much more attention from top management.

The importance of these markets will inevitably be reflected in the ethnic and national origin of senior management. At present, with a few exceptions such as Citicorp and Unilever, senior management ranks are filled with nationals from the company's home country. By the year 2010, however, the top 200 managers from around the world for any multinational will have a much greater cultural and ethnic mix.

How many of today's multinationals are prepared to accommodate 30% to 40% of their top team of 200 coming from China, India, and Brazil? How will that cultural mix influence decision making, risk taking, and team building? Diversity will put an enormous burden on top-level managers to articulate clearly the values and behaviors

{ 49 }

expected of senior managers, and it will demand large investments in training and socialization. The need for a single company culture will also become more critical as people from different cultures begin to work together. Providing the right glue to hold companies together will be a big challenge.

That challenge will be intensified by an impending power shift within multinationals. The end of corporate imperialism suggests more than a new relationship between the developed and the emerging economies. It also suggests an end to the era of centralized corporate power—embodied in the attitude that headquarters knows best—and a shift to a much more dispersed base of power and influence.

Consider the new patterns of knowledge transfer we are beginning to see. Unilever, for example, is transferring Indian managers with experience in low-cost distribution to China, where they will build a national distribution system and train Chinese managers. And it has transferred Indian managers with knowledge of tier-two markets to Brazil. The phenomenon of using managers from outside the home country to transfer knowledge is relatively new. It will grow over time to the point where the multinational becomes an organization with several centers of expertise and excellence.

Multinationals will be shaped by a wide variety of forces in the coming decades. The big emerging markets will be one of the major forces they come up against. And the effect will be nothing short of dramatic change on both sides. They will challenge each other to change for the better as a truly global economy takes shape in the twenty-first century. The MNCs will create a higher standard of products, quality, technology, and management practices. Large, opaque markets will gradually become more transparent. The process of transition to market economies will be evolutionary, uneven, and fraught with uncertainties. But the direction is no longer in question.

In order to participate effectively in the big emerging markets, multinationals will increasingly have to reconfigure their resource bases, rethink their cost structures, redesign their product development processes, and challenge their assumptions about the cultural mix of their top managers. In short, they will have to develop a new mindset and adopt new business models to achieve global competitiveness in the postimperialist age.

EXHIBIT 1

Market size

Emerging markets versus the United States

Product	China	India	Brazil	United States
televisions (million units)	13.6	5.2	7.8	23.0
detergent (kilograms per person)	2.5	2.7	7.3	14.4
(million tons)	3.5	2.3	1.1	3.9
shampoo ($ billions)	1.0	0.8	1.0	1.5
pharmaceuticals ($ billions)	5.0	2.8	8.0	60.6
automotive (million units)	1.6	0.7	2.1	15.5
power (megawatt capacity)	236,542	81,736	59,950	810,964

EXHIBIT 2

The Market Pyramid in China, India, and Brazil

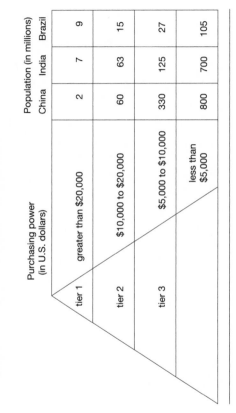

Purchasing power (in U.S. dollars)	Population (in millions)		
	China	India	Brazil
tier 1 — greater than $20,000	2	7	9
tier 2 — $10,000 to $20,000	60	63	15
tier 3 — $5,000 to $10,000	330	125	27
less than $5,000	800	700	105

{ 55 }

ABOUT THE AUTHORS

C.K. Prahalad is the Paul and Ruth Mc-Cracken Distinguished University Professor of Corporate Strategy at the University of Michigan's Ross School of Business.

Kenneth Lieberthal is a professor of political science, the William Davidson Professor of Business Administration, and a distinguished fellow and director for China at the William Davidson Institute at the University of Michigan.

ALSO BY THESE AUTHORS

C.K. Prahalad

Harvard Business Review Articles

"Cocreating Business's New Social Compact"
with Jeb Brugmann

"Staying Ahead of Your Competition"
with Gary Hamel and Liisa Valikangas

"Strategic Intent"
with Gary Hamel

"Serving the World's Poor, Profitably"
with Allen Hammond

Harvard Business Press Books

The Future of Competition: Co-Creating Unique Value with Customers
with Venkatram Ramaswamy

Competing for the Future
with Gary Hamel

Kenneth Lieberthal

Harvard Business Review Articles

"Scorched Earth: Will Environmental Risks in China Overwhelm Its Opportunities?"
with Elizabeth Economy

Article Summary

The Idea in Brief

Hundreds of millions of people in China, India, Indonesia, and Brazil are eager to enter the marketplace. Yet multinational companies (MNCs) typically pitch their products to emerging markets' tiny segment of affluent buyers—who most resemble Westerners. Why? They think of developing countries simply as new places to sell their old products. Thanks to this imperialist mind-set, MNCs miss out on much larger markets further down the socioeconomic pyramid—which local rivals snap up.

How to seize this opportunity? **Don't assume you can export your current business model around the world.** Coca-Cola initially lost market share to Pepsi in India by using its traditional advertising strategies instead of tailoring campaigns to local markets. **Reconfigure your resources.** Look to emerging markets for technical talent, as multinationals Philips and ABB have done in hiring more Asian employees while shrinking their European workforces. And **reengineer cost structures** to *profitably* serve less-affluent consumers. For example, Fiat designed a popular $9,000 car specifically for less affluent Brazilians.

By competing innovatively in developing countries, as companies such as Coca-Cola, Gillette, General Electric, and Boeing have done, you'll unlock major new sources of revenue for your business.

The Idea in Practice

To compete innovatively in emerging markets, consider these questions:

How Can You Best Serve Developing Regions' Emerging Middle Classes?

To win them, rethink:

- *Customer perceptions of value.* Chinese, for example, have snapped up Philips Electronics' video-CD player, deeming it a great two-for-one bargain—though there's no Western market for the product.

- *Brand management.* For example, Coca-Cola recaptured Indian market share from Pepsi by modifying its brand message. How? It used local heroes in its advertising.

- *Market-building costs.* Changing regional habits is difficult and expensive. For example,

instead of trying to convince Chinese consumers to use mobile phones, Motorola
accommodated their preference for pagers
by developing pagers that could display
longer text messages.

- *Product design and packaging.* Indians, for
  example, prefer single-serve packets (for
  products as varied as shampoo, pickles,
  and cough syrup) because they can buy
  only what they need, experiment, and conserve cash.

How Do Local Distribution Systems Work?

In China, distribution is regulated by local and
provincial governments, and Chinese joint-venture
partners protect their turf. But in India, individual
entrepreneurs control a national distribution system
through long-standing arrangements with small-
scale distributors and banks. The lesson? Don't
assume you'll have easy access to distribution—or

that distribution works the same way abroad as it does at home.

Should You Use Expatriate or Local Leaders?

Expatriates from an MNC's host country can transfer technology and ensure that local employees conform to the corporate culture. But many aren't willing to stay long enough to fully understand local nuances and leverage their learning. Native-born leaders also offer advantages—such as appreciation of local nuances and deep commitment to native markets. But they may lack a sufficiently strong voice at corporate headquarters to convey their knowledge. Blend expatriate and local leadership to capture global knowledge while honoring local sensitivities.

Should Your Overseas Business Units Act Uniformly or Independently?

There's no one right answer. In markets with massive governmental interference (think China), coordinate business units so they comply with government priorities (such as local sourcing agreements), even though this is taxing and time consuming. In markets with less-restrictive governments, business units may operate more autonomously.

What Role Should Local Partners Play?

Joint ventures pose problems if parties have different expectations about what each will provide, who controls what, and how soon the profits will roll in. Local partners often lack adequate market knowledge or use archaic business practices. If so, limit reliance on local partners—or use them as figureheads who can provide a local face.